Getting To Know
Your Goldfish

Getting To Know Your Goldfish

Gill Page

INTERPET PUBLISHING

The Author

Gill Page has been involved with a wide variety of animals for many years. She has run a successful pet centre and for some time helped in rescuing and re-homing unwanted animals. She has cared for many animals of her own and is keen to pass on her experience so that children may learn how to look after their pets lovingly and responsibly.

Published by Interpet Publishing,
Vincent Lane,
Dorking,
Surrey RH4 3YX,
England

ISBN 1-84286-089-5

The recommendations in this book are given without any guarantees on the part of the author and publisher. If in doubt, seek the advice of a vet or pet-care specialist.

Credits

Editor: Philip de Ste. Croix

Designer: Phil Clucas MSIAD

Studio photography: Neil Sutherland

Colour artwork: Rod Ferring

Production management: Consortium, Poslingford, Suffolk

Print production: Sino Publishing House Ltd., Hong Kong

Printed and bound in China

Contents

Making Friends   6

My First Home   8

An "All-in-One" House   10

Decorating My House   12

My Own Garden   14

Plastic Plants   16

Choosing Me   18

My First Day At Home   20

Keeping My House Clean   22

Toys and Playthings   24

My Favourite Food   26

Treats and Titbits   28

Visits To My Doctor   30

Living With Friends   32

Safety in the Home   34

Holiday Care   36

My Special Page   38

Goldfish Check List   39

Common Goldfish   40

Comets and Shubunkins   42

Other Fancy Goldfish   44

A Note To Parents   46

Acknowledgements   48

Making Friends

Hello. I am your new friend. What is your name? I need a name too. I am not very clever, so I will not learn to come when you call, but I will know when you are talking to me. I am going to tell you a few things about myself and then you will understand how to take really good care of me.

I spend all my time swimming around in my tank. It can be very boring if I only have a small house. I don't need a bed to sleep in as I can rest in the water.

I cannot keep my house clean on my own, so you will have to help me. You must keep my water fresh and clean. I like to be fed every day, but I will not need extra water to drink, will I?

I am a quiet friend as I cannot talk to you, but I will soon know who you are. You can put fish toys in my house to give me interesting things to look at and some plants for me to hide in. I just know we are going to be very good friends.

I can see all around me without turning my head. You can't do that, can you?

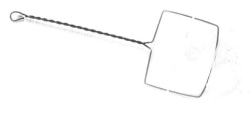

My First Home

Before you can choose me and take me home, you must get my new house ready for me. You can buy a "starter kit". This is a tank that has all the bits and pieces you will need to make my new home cosy for me. First there will be a good-sized plastic tank. I really hate swimming in small round bowls. I get quite giddy having to swim round and round in circles. There will be a net for you to catch me. You will not be able to hold me in your hands – I am very slippery and you might drop me. A packet of food will be included so that you can feed me as soon as I arrive.

I swim through the tunnel to visit my other house.

To help you keep my house clean you will need to use a
filter. The starter kit will have an easy one for you to use.
Follow the instructions that tell you how to fit it into the
tank. You must ask a grown-up to help you do this; it is
electric and will have to be plugged into a wall socket and
you should not do this on your own. Cover the bottom of
the tank with some gravel. Wash the gravel before you use
it. You can do this with a sieve, a bucket and some fresh
water. Fill the tank to the top with fresh, clean water.

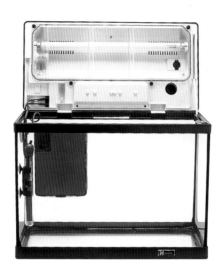

An "All-in-One" House

An "all-in-one tank" costs more money, but it has the filter and a heater already fixed in it. Put gravel in the tank in the same way as you did with the starter tank. It should be about 8cm (3in) deep. Press it down with your hands and make it a little higher at the back and slope it down to the front of the tank. Slowly fill up the tank with water from the cold water tap. You must pour the water in very slowly or it will make a mess of all the gravel and stir up dirt in the water. Putting a small plate onto the gravel and pouring the water on to the plate helps to keep the water clean. Take out the plate when the tank is full. Ask a grown-up to help if you cannot reach.

You should now add some water conditioner. This is a special liquid that makes the tap water safe for me to live in. Read the directions on the bottle first. Turn on the filter and put in some plants and rocks – I tell you how to do this on the next four pages. Leave the tank for two days to settle down before you choose me and bring me home to put me in to my new house.

My owner is fitting a filter to help keep my water clean.

My filter must be under water before you switch it on.

Decorating
My House

The gravel you use in my house need not be the
ordinary brown stuff. It can be almost any colour.
I think blue stones are pretty. Half-fill a sieve with
gravel, hold it over a bucket and pour clean water over
the stones. Keep doing this until the gravel is clean.
Put the gravel in the tank. Wash some larger stones;
you can use them to make me a cave to hide in, but
be sure that it will not fall down or it might squash me.
There are some lovely coloured stones that you can
buy. We could pretend that they are jewels and that
there is treasure at the bottom of my tank.

Buy some pieces of special aquarium wood, wash them carefully under the tap and then push them into the gravel. I can play hide and seek with my friends around and through them. You can also use sea shells to make my house look different. Wash the shells really well to clean out any salt that may be left inside them. To make my house look more exciting, you could fix a special poster to the back of the tank. You can buy them from pet shops. There are all sorts of pictures to choose from, or try painting one yourself.

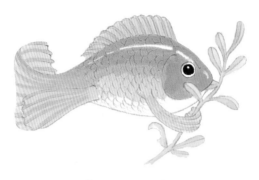

My Own Garden

To make my house even nicer, I would like some plants growing in it. I can hide behind them and, when you are not looking, I can eat them! It will feel as if I have a garden and a snack bar too. The pet shop will be able to show you the best plants to grow in my tank. The plants must look clean and the leaves be bright green. Don't choose plants that have lots of yellow or brown leaves – I don't want those in my house. I am very fussy, you know.

There is one problem that the plants have – their names are often very hard to say. One of the best is *Elodea*. It helps to keep my water fresh and it is good to eat. Other plants are Hornwort (*Ceratophyllum*) and Arrowhead (*Sagittaria*). *Elodea* is sold in little bunches. Tie a stone to the bottom of the bunch and bury it into the gravel. Other plants will be sold in little pots. Plant them into the gravel. I can be very naughty and dig them up if they are not planted deep enough! Put the plants into the tank when it is only half-full of water, then finish filling it up.

Plastic Plants

Sometimes I can be very naughty. I might start digging the real plants up and I may even chew them into little bits. If I start doing this, you can buy plastic plants instead that I cannot harm. Some look just like real plants. Until I try to eat them, I think they are real too! They come in different sizes. Put the small ones at the front of the tank. The taller ones go at the back. You still have to plant them into the gravel to keep them in one place. There are some that are the same shape as real ones, but they are blue, red, pink, yellow or white. They make my house look really colourful.

We were kept as pets by Chinese and Japanese people hundreds of years ago.

These pretend plants will last a long time, but they may start to look dirty after a while and then you will have to take them out of my tank to clean them. Use warm water and a small brush to scrub them. Do not use soap or any other cleaner as this will make me feel ill when you put them back into my house. When you have washed them under the tap, scoop out a jugful of water from my tank and soak the plastic plants in this water for a while. This will wash away any traces of chlorine in the tap water.

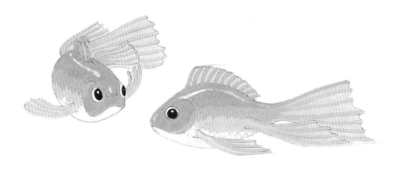

Choosing Me

You can choose me from a pet shop, a fish breeder, or you can even ask your local animal rescue centre if they have any friends like me that need a new home. There will be lots of us swimming around in a tank. See that we all look clean and that our fins are not torn nor do they have white spots on them. My skin should look bright and shiny, and my eyes clear. My tank needs to be clean and the water must be clear.

Do not buy me if there are any dead fish in the tank.
I will be sick too. I should be whizzing around the tank,
not sitting still on the bottom. If I am floating on the
surface of the water, it means I am not very well. Never
buy me if any of the other fish are doing these things,
even if I look fine. It is best to buy me when I am still
quite small. I should be no bigger than 8cm (3in) long.
When you have chosen me, the helper in the pet shop
will catch me in a special net. That is when you can
see how fast I can swim!

*Ready to go home. The bottom of the bag is taped
so that I cannot get stuck in the corner.*

A thermometer shows how warm or cold my water is.

86 30
84 29
82 28
81 27
79 26
77 25
75 24
73 23
72 22
70 21
68 20
66 19
°F °C

My First Day At Home

When I have been caught, I will be popped into a plastic bag for the journey home. It will be half-full of water that has been taken from my tank. This will make me feel safe as you take me home. The top is tied with an elastic band so that I can't fall out. Put the plastic bag into a box or pet carrier. See that I do not get too hot or too cold. I do not want to be bounced about too much either. I will feel sea sick.

My new house should be ready for me when we get home. Gently put me – still in the tied-up bag – into the water of the tank. It will float on the top. Leave me floating for 20 minutes. This allows the temperature of the water in my bag to become the same as the water in the tank. You know what a shock it is when you get into water that is just too hot or too cold. I feel the same. Then open the top of the bag. Scoop some of the tank water into a jug and pour it gently into the bag. Wait for another five minutes so that the water can mix, then push down the side of the bag. I will swim out into my new home.

Do not use soap, detergent or disinfectant to clean my tank.

Keeping My House Clean

I like my house to be kept clean. A filter will help, but you will still have to change some water every week. Use a special bucket to keep water in, just for me. I hate water that has come straight from the tap. Never use the hot water tap. Fill the bucket with cold water and add fish water conditioner. Ask a grown-up how much to use.

The two halves of the magnetic cleaner stick together through the glass. Moving it up and down cleans away the dirt.

Turn off the filter and the light – if you have one. Take the
lid off the tank and wipe it with a clean cloth. Scrape off
any green slime on the inside of the glass. Use a suction
pump to clean the gravel and pump out the dirty water into
another bucket. No more than about 10 per cent of the
water, mind you. Ask a grown-up to work this out for you
if the sums are a bit hard. Take out the filter. Pull off the
outside and wash it. If the filter has a sponge, wash it in
some water you have taken out of the tank. If it has a
throw-away filter, replace it with a new one. Put the filter
together and put it back in the tank. Use a jug to fill up
the tank with the clean water from my special bucket.

Toys and Playthings

There are a lot of toys that you can put in my tank. I don't play with them, but I enjoy swimming in and around new things. There are divers that stay on the bottom and some even go up and down. Treasure chests are very exciting, but they sometimes have pretend octopuses or crabs on them – scary. Sometimes there are sunken ships – they are fun. You can put in some large rocks, but not if I have large bubble eyes – I could bump my eyes on the sharp bits of stone. One of my favourite toys is a "No Fishing" sign!

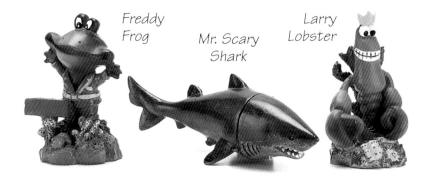

Freddy Frog

Mr. Scary Shark

Larry Lobster

I do not like too many toys in my house as I keep bumping into them. Only put two or three in. You can change them around from time to time. You can buy some wooden ornaments that are made just for me, but never, ever, use wood from the garden or the tool shed. It could make the water bad for me. I might even die. There are some really funny fishy friends to share my house. I just love Freddy Frog and Larry Lobster. To give your friends a real fright you could fix the two halves of Mr. Scary Shark to the inside and outside of my tank. It looks as if he is escaping clean out of the tank!

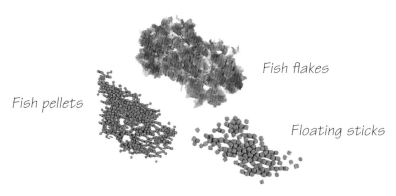

Fish flakes

Fish pellets

Floating sticks

My Favourite Food

I am a small pet friend. I do not need a lot of food, but I still must be fed every day. A tiny pinch of dry food, that I quickly gobble up, will be enough. Sprinkle it on to the water. Don't use too much or it will turn my water smelly and clog the filter. The dried food comes in flakes or little pellets. When I am very small, the flakes are easy for me to eat. As I grow, you can use the pellets. The ones called "Floating Sticks" stay on the top of the water. When I have finished eating, scoop the spare sticks out of the tank, and throw them away.

I should be able to gobble up my food in just a minute or two.

Having some real plants in my house will give me something to nibble between meals. I will rush to the front of my house every time I see you, hoping you will feed me. Talk to me then, but remember only to feed me at mealtimes. Too much food will make me ill.

Feeding Timetable

I like to have my food at the same time every day. I will know if you are late. You don't have to give me lunch. I just have two meals a day – a tiny pinch of food for each meal. If you give me too much, the leftovers sink to the bottom of my tank where it makes the water very smelly.

Breakfast
One pinch of
flakes or sticks.

Supper
One pinch of
flakes or floating
sticks.

Once a week
give me a treat –
see page 28 –
instead of my
dried food.

Dried bloodworm

Treats and Titbits

I don't eat huge meals, but I do like a treat once or twice a week. The one I enjoy best of all is called "Daphnia". Another name for it is water flea, but it isn't a flea really. There are also some tiny, red worms that you can feed to me. They are called "bloodworms". You can buy these fresh, frozen or dried. I like them all. Only give me a tiny pinch. Always buy these from a really clean shop. You will only need to buy a little at a time so it remains fresh. Old and stale food is bad for me.

You may not like the thought of eating water fleas, but I think they are yummy!

To find my food I will look for it with my eyes and I can smell it too.

Never dig up worms from the garden as food for me. There may be horrid stuff in the earth where they come from. It could even kill me. Do not catch any water fleas from ponds. The water may be bad and that will harm me too. I will be very happy when you come to see me as I always think you are going to feed me. I have forgotten that I have just eaten. It should only take me one minute to finish my food or treat. If it takes any longer, you have given me too much!

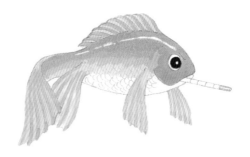

Visits To My Doctor

My doctor is called a veterinarian. Vet for short. My vet helps to keep me feeling well and looks after me when I am sick. Check me every day. Am I swimming happily all around my house? If I am sitting on the bottom of my tank or swimming round and round in small circles, I may be sick. Look at my skin and fins. Are there any little white spots on them? I could have an illness called fish fungus. This will look as if I have bits of cotton wool stuck on me.

My tank water is being tested by the vet to show how clean it is.

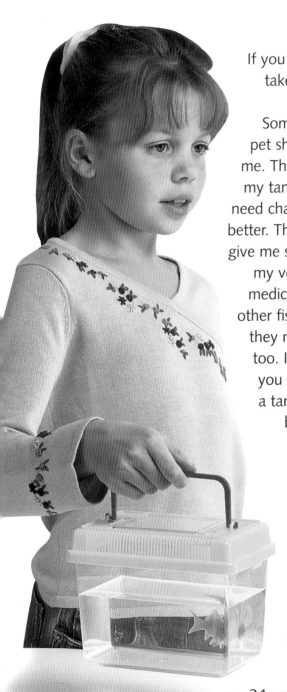

If you think I do not look well, take me to my doctor in a small, plastic tank. Sometimes the people in a pet shop may be able to help me. They can test the water in my tank. The water may just need changing to make me feel better. They will also be able to give me some medicines but only my vet can give me strong medicines. If I am living with other fishy friends when I fall ill, they may need to see the vet too. If I am the only sick fish, you will have to put me into a tank on my own until I get better. This is called a quarantine tank.

You can take me to the vet in my own small tank.

I like to have other fish in my tank to keep me company.

Living With Friends

I really do not like living on my own. I know we will be good friends and that you will enjoy watching me, but I will still need another fishy friend to live with me. The easiest thing is to buy two of us at the same time from the same place. Then I will not be lonely when you are not there. If the tank is large, you will be able to keep more than two of us. A tank that is 30cm (12in) wide, 40cm (15in) deep, and 60cm (24in) long can have four or five of us living in it. We will have lots of room to play. It also gives us space for when we get bigger.

Begin with two goldfish like me. After two weeks you could add different fish, like a shubunkin or a sarasa. If you wait another two weeks, you can add a really fancy fish. Choose a fantail or an oranda. This gives the filter in my tank time to soak up all the dirt in the water. You may have other pet friends living with you – but you must never leave me alone with them in the room. They might try to eat me.

Safety in the Home

I am not very good at looking after myself. When I am in my tank I feel safe, but I need you to take good care of me. My house is very heavy when it is full of water. Please make sure that it is put on a strong shelf or table.
I do not like my house standing next to a window or room heater. The water in my tank could get too hot.
If the tank is in a draught, I could get too cold. Ask grown-ups not to use spray cans near me. Furniture polish, fly spray and even hair spray can hurt me.

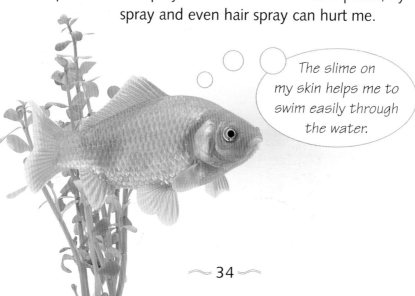

The slime on my skin helps me to swim easily through the water.

Never let anybody bang on the side of my tank. It will send shock waves through the water and harm me. If you have to catch me, always use my own net. Scoop me up in it. Try not to squash me against the glass or pinch me with the edge of the fishing net. Always put a lid on my house. This will stop anything falling in. It will also stop other pets like cats from trying to scoop me out. Wash your hands after touching my tank water or anything in it.

Holiday Care

I need someone to look after me when you are away from home. Are you only going to be away for one or two days? If so, you can pop a small tablet of holiday food into the water that will keep me going while you are away. Pet shops sell them. The tablet slowly melts in the water. I can nibble it whenever I feel hungry. If you are going to be away for longer than two days, you must ask a friend to feed and care for me. The easiest thing to do is to leave me at home and ask your friend to visit. I must be fed every day and some of my water will need changing every week.

*Our holiday home is great, but we don't
want to stay in here for too long.*

Or I could go to live with friends while you are away.
Don't try to move my big tank; it's easier to put me
into a smaller one for the holiday. There's only room
for two of us in a smaller house like this. Put some
plants, gravel and decorations in it to make me feel
at home. Ask a grown-up to put a special fish water
conditioner into my tank. It helps to keep me well
while you are away. Leave the phone number of my
vet or the local pet/aquatic shop. They will be able
to help if I become sick while you are away.

My Special Page

My name is

My birthday is

My favourite food is

My favourite snack is

What sort of fish am I?

My best hiding place is

What colour am I?

How long are my fins?

My vet's telephone number is

Please put a
photograph or a
picture of me
here

Goldfish Check List

Every day
1 If I have a light in my tank, turn it on in the morning and off at night.
2 Check that the filter is working.
3 Feed me.

Every week
4 Clean the bottom of the tank with a gravel cleaner.
5 Scrape off any green slime on the tank.
6 Change some of the water in my tank.
7 Tidy the plants in my tank.
8 Wash the filter.

Every year
9 Move everything around in my tank.
10 Ask a grown-up to check any electrical units in my house to make sure they are working properly.

Once a year take all the gravel out of my tank and wash it well.

Common Goldfish

I am the easiest of your goldfish friends to care for. I am mostly a bright, golden-orange colour. I can also be a pale yellow or silver. When I was a baby, I was a very dull colour. My scales were greeny-brown. Some of my brothers and sisters were black. The dull colours help us to hide from other bigger fish. They will eat us if they see us. Even our parents may think we are food. We look like this until we are about six months old. Then we slowly change from being very dull to bright and shiny gold.

A common goldfish, like me, can grow to be about 40cm (16in) long.

I have round dark eyes. I do not have eyelids, so I cannot close my eyes as you do. I sleep at night by resting near the bottom of my tank. I can grow quite big. I may grow too big for my house. I could then live in an outdoor pond. I am a hardy fish so I am able to live outdoors. The garden pond must be at least 80cm (30in) deep. Ask a grown-up to help you move me. If you have very, very cold winters, I mustn't be left outside. Bring me indoors to live in a tank until the weather is warmer.

Comets and Shubunkins

Some of us are known as fancy goldfish. I may be the same shape as a goldfish or look very different. I can be a plain gold or a mix of all sorts of colours. If I am a comet, I will look just like a goldfish, but I will have a long trailing tail. I am a comet tail sarasa, and my body is silvery white and I have patches of golden orange. I have a long tail and fins. I look very beautiful as I swim around in my house, but I can really speed through the water. See if you can catch me.

My tail helps to push me through the water.

*I am called a shubunkin, and my skin has lots
of different colours all mixed up together.*

My pals the shubunkins are also the same shape as a
common goldfish. Shubunkins are amazing multicoloured
fish. They are covered in splodges of white, blue, gold,
brown, red and silver. All the colours are mixed up
together on their bodies. There are lots of black spots
all over their skin and fins. Common goldfish, comets,
sarasas and shubunkins all live happily together in the
same house. If you like, you can put us into a garden
pond for the summer. Bring us back into our tank indoors
for the winter. We do not like icy cold water. Brr!

Other Fancy Goldfish

I may have a fat, round body with a long, floaty tail and fins. I will be called a fantail. My colour is red or sometimes red and white. If I have lots of different colours on my body, I will be called a calico fantail. Another fishy friend is the same shape as a fantail, but he has bobbly skin on his head. He is called an oranda. Another friend looks very like the oranda, but doesn't have a fin on the top of his back. He is called a lionhead.

We are fantails. We use our fins to help us glide through the water.

I also have some really weird fish friends. The black moor is a velvety black colour, with a long tail and fins. He has eyes which stick out sideways from his head. My friend the bubble-eyed fish has huge bubbly eyes. Bubble-eyed fish do not like pieces of rock, plastic plants or toys in their house. They can scratch their eyes on sharp, pointy bits. They cannot see very well either. Always feed them with food that floats on the surface of the water. They miss the food if it falls to the bottom and will end up feeling very hungry. They must always live indoors.

I am a bubble-eyed fish. I don't see very well.
Where did all the food go?

A Note To Parents

Having pets is fun and the relationship between child and pet is a magical one. I hope this book will encourage the new, young pet owner to look after their pet responsibly and enjoyably. Obviously parents will have to play a supervisory role, both in daily care and to explain that the new pet is a living being and not a toy. A well-cared-for pet is a happy one. Fish are relatively undemanding pets. They don't need exercising and are very quiet. They do require regular feeding and may even learn to take food from the hand. Water quality is important too. The simple act of overfeeding can poison the water.

Some of the subjects covered in this book may seem over-simplified to an adult, but I have tried to avoid too much technical detail. Parents may need to oversee water changes and tank maintenance. Always purchase the fish from reputable aquatic centres or breeders. Fish that have been subjected to stress due to overcrowding, lack of food or poor water quality will be susceptible to disease. Check that the fish have been quarantined before being released for sale. Good aquatic centres are usually happy to give advice and help to the novice fish keeper.

Acknowledgements

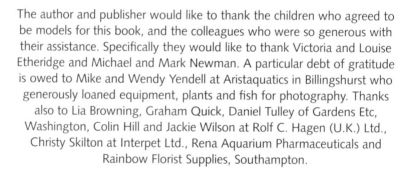

The author and publisher would like to thank the children who agreed to be models for this book, and the colleagues who were so generous with their assistance. Specifically they would like to thank Victoria and Louise Etheridge and Michael and Mark Newman. A particular debt of gratitude is owed to Mike and Wendy Yendell at Aristaquatics in Billingshurst who generously loaned equipment, plants and fish for photography. Thanks also to Lia Browning, Graham Quick, Daniel Tulley of Gardens Etc, Washington, Colin Hill and Jackie Wilson at Rolf C. Hagen (U.K.) Ltd., Christy Skilton at Interpet Ltd., Rena Aquarium Pharmaceuticals and Rainbow Florist Supplies, Southampton.

Thanks are due to Geoff Rogers of Ideas into Print and Damion Diplock of the RSPCA Photolibrary who kindly supplied some of the photographs that are reproduced in this book.
RSPCA Photolibrary: 1, 3 (Joe B. Blossom)
6-7, 46, 47 (Angela Hampton), 15, 43, 45 (Dave Bevan)